Wir produzieren nachhaltig
- Klimaneutrales Produkt
- Papiere aus nachhaltigen und kontrollierten Quellen
- Hergestellt in Europa

FSC www.fsc.org MIX Papier | Fördert gute Waldnutzung FSC® C002795

Wir haben die Wahl! – Internationale Cartoons zu Demokratie und Rechtsstaat

Zweisprachige Ausgabe

1. Auflage 2024

– Originalausgabe –

ISBN 978-3-8303-3682-2

Herausgegeben von Christian Langer

Übersetzung ins Englische oder Deutsche: Jessica Link

Redaktion Texte: Clara Sieveking, LCI

Redaktion und Lektorat: Antje Haubner und Jessica Link

Herstellung: Monika Swirski

Cover: Monika Swirski unter Verwendung eines Cartoons von Dorthe Landschulz

Cartoon Backcover: Dario Castillejos

WIR HABEN DIE WAHL!

Internationale Cartoons zu Demokratie und Rechtsstaat

Mit Beiträgen von **Oby Ezekwesili, Mikołaj Pietrzak, Homeira Qaderi, Yésica Sánchez Maya**

Herausgegeben von **Christian Langer**

Mit Cartoons von **Amorim, Frank Bahr,** Harm Bengen, Camille Besse, Bettina Bexte, BURKH, Chapatte, Darío Castillejos, Doaa Eladl, Rod Emmerson, Tim Oliver Feicke, **Fares Garabet,** Damien Glez, Katharina Greve, Markus Grolik, Teresa Habild, Osama Hajjaj, Ruth Hebler, Michael Holtschulte, Björn Karnebogen, Musa Kart, Petra Kaster, **Vladimir Kazanevsky,** Arkadiusz Krupa, **Manjul,** Dorthe Landschulz, Mario Lars, Til Mette, Denis Metz, MOCK, OL, Ted Rall, Stephan Rürup, Heiko Sakurai, Schwarwel, Swen, Klaus Stuttman, Stefano Tartarotti, Bas van der Schot, Cathy Wilcox

LAWCOM INSTITUTE

LAPPAN

»... and the constitutional state was very sad because more and more people were too stupid for it.«

CHRISTIAN LANGER

Christian Langer, Jahrgang 1958, glücklicher Ehemann, Vater und Großvater, Kommunikationswissenschaftler und als Journalist tätig für Tageszeitungen, Magazine, Hörfunk und Fernsehen. Seit 1990 Inhaber einer Beratungsagentur für integrierte Kommunikationsberatung und Public Affairs. 2022 Mitgründer des LawCom.Institute, das sich aktiv für Rechtsstaatlichkeit und Demokratie einsetzt.

LawCom.Institute

Ein demokratischer Rechtsstaat ist die beste Grundlage für eine faire und gute Zukunft, national und international. Auf der Grundlage dieser gemeinsamen Überzeugung hat Christian Langer, Jahrgang 1958, mit Jan Curschmann und Friedrich-Joachim Mehmel 2022 das LawCom.Institute gegründet. Mit dem Ziel, für Rechtsstaatlichkeit und Demokratie aktiv zu werben und beides gegen Angriffe zu verteidigen.

Christian Langer (born in 1958) is a happy husband, father and grandfather who works as a communication expert and journalist for daily newspapers, magazines, and broadcasting services. Since 1990, he has been running an agency for integrated communications and public affairs. In 2022 he co-founded the LawCom. Institute which actively promotes the rule of law and democracy.

LawCom.Institute

A democratic constitutional state is the best basis for a fair and good future, both nationally and internationally. Based on this shared belief, Christian Langer founded the LawCom.Institute together with Jan Curschmann and Friedrich-Joachim Mehmel in 2022 with the aim of actively promoting and defending the rule of law and democracy.

DRAW ATTENTION 2024: HERAUSGEBERWORT / EDITOR'S FOREWORD

Cartoonist:innen kommen auf den Punkt, ohne Umschweife, direkt, schonungslos, ehrlich, entwaffnend. Sie berühren uns, sie regen uns auf, sie fordern uns heraus. Mit ein paar Federstrichen lassen sie eine neue Sicht der Welt entstehen. Sie bürsten gegen den Strich – mit dem Strich ihrer Zeichnungen. Ihre Kunst ist dem Augenblick verpflichtet und wirkt nachhaltig. Ein Stift, ein Stück Papier, ein Tablet. Mehr braucht es nicht, um die Sicht auf die Welt zu verändern.

»Wir haben die Wahl! Internationale Cartoons zu Demokratie und Rechtsstaat« nutzt die aufrührerische Kraft der Karikatur. Künstler:innen aus allen fünf Kontinenten haben ihre Kreativität und Leidenschaft eingesetzt, um Aufmerksamkeit zu schaffen und ein Zeichen zu setzen: für Demokratie und Rechtsstaat!

Mal witzig-ironisch, mal derb-kraftvoll, mal poetisch-verspielt. Sie stoßen vor den Kopf, sie ecken an. Nur eines tun sie nicht: Sie lassen uns nicht kalt.

Cartoons sind Wahrheiten, die die Welt braucht, um nicht im Brei der wohlgefälligen Relativierung zu vergessen, worum es im Kern geht: um die wahrhaftige Auseinandersetzung um den richtigen Weg.

»Wir haben die Wahl! Internationale Cartoons zu Demokratie und Rechtsstaat« ist unmissverständlich, ist parteiisch, ist subjektiv. Und steht für eine gemeinsame Haltung: wachzurütteln, Gedanken zu provozieren, Meinungen zu ändern, Engagement zu schaffen.

Allen, die »Wir haben die Wahl!« mit Leben erfüllt haben, gilt unser Dank: den Künstler:innen, den Essayist:innen Oby Ezekwesili, Yésica Sánchez Maya, Mikołaj Pietrzak und Homeira Qaderi sowie dem Team des Lappan Verlages und des LawCom. Institute.

Wenn Sie dieses Vorwort gelesen haben, hat »Wir haben die Wahl!« Wort gehalten, es hat Aufmerksamkeit geweckt. Für die Cartoons, für die Gedanken der Essayist:innen und vor allem für die gemeinsame Überzeugung: Demokratie und Rechtsstaat sind unersetzlich für eine gute Zukunft dieser Welt!

Cartoonists get straight to the point: they are direct, unsparing, honest, and disarming. They move us. They upset us. They challenge us. With just a few strokes, they create a new view of the world. With their drawings, they strive against the stream. Their art captures the moment with a lasting effect. A pencil, a piece of paper or a tablet, that's all it takes to change the way we see the world.

»Draw Attention! International Cartoonists for Democracy and the Rule of Law« uses the incendiary power of caricature. With their creativity and passion, artists from all five continents attract attention to and make a statement for democracy and the rule of law!

Their cartoons are sometimes witty and ironic, sometimes crude and powerful, and sometimes poetically playful. They offend. They scandalise. However, there's one thing they don't do: they don't leave us cold.

Cartoons are truths the world needs so that amid a pleasing relativization we don't forget what it is all about: an honest debate about the right path.

»Draw Attention! International Cartoonists for Democracy and the Rule of Law« is unambiguous, partisan, and subjective. It stands for a common approach: we want to shake things up, provoke thoughts, change opinions, and create commitment.

We would like to thank everyone who brought »Draw Attention!« to life: the artists, the essayists Oby Ezekwesili, Yésica Sánchez Maya, Mikołaj Pietrzak, and Homeira Qaderi, as well as the teams at Lappan Verlag and LawCom.Institute.

If you have read this foreword, »Draw Attention!« has kept its word. It has drawn attention to the cartoons, to the thoughts of the essayists and, above all, to our shared belief: democracy and the rule of law are irreplaceable for a good future of this world!

»With this attack, the police doesn't exclude an antisemitic background.«

»We have already hidden a Jew in our basement
so we don't have to blame ourselves in the future.«

»This news text contains the word »AfD« three times. Isn't there another word for it?«
»Nazis.«

AfD (Alternative für Deutschland/Alternative for Germany) is the biggest right-wing political party in Germany. Some of its members have an extreme right-wing background.

LA PROMESA

Das Versprechen The Promise

CAMINO ELECTORAL

Weg zu den Wahlen Path to the Elections

ABRIENDO CAMINO

Den Weg bahnen   Paving the Way

YÉSICA SÁNCHEZ MAYA

Yésica Sánchez Maya, ein wichtiges Mitglied des Consorcio para el Diálogo Parlamentario y la Equidad Oaxaca, ist eine bekannte Menschenrechtsverteidigerin in Oaxaca, Mexiko. Für ihren unermüdlichen Einsatz wurde sie auf dem Internationalen Tag der Menschenrechte 2020 ausgezeichnet. Als Spezialistin für strategische Rechtsstreitigkeiten konzentriert sich Yésica auf indigene Rechte, soziale Proteste und geschlechtsspezifische Gewalt. Seit 2008 leitet sie das Programm zum Aufbau sozialer Bewegungen. In der Vergangenheit war sie unter anderem Präsidentin der Liga Mexicana de Derechos Humanos Limeddh-Oaxaca und wurde für ihre Führungsrolle im Bereich der Menschenrechte ausgezeichnet.

Yésica Sánchez Maya, a key member of *Consorcio para el Diálogo Parlamentario y la Equidad Oaxaca,* is a distinguished human rights defender in Oaxaca, Mexico. In recognition of her tireless efforts, she received an honorable mention during the 2020 International Human Rights Day. As a specialist in strategic litigation, Yésica focuses on indigenous rights, social protest issues, and gender-based violence. Since 2008 she has led the Social Movement Construction Program. Her past roles include serving as the President of Liga Mexicana de Derechos Humanos Limeddh-Oaxaca and she has received awards for her human rights leadership.

Consorcio Oaxaca ist eine feministische Menschenrechtsorganisation, die sich seit 2011 für Menschenrechte stark macht und Missstände anprangert. Dafür werden wir angegriffen und eingeschüchtert. Aber wir hören nicht auf, Gewalt gegen Frauen und die gravierende Menschenrechtskrise in unserem Land zu dokumentieren und das Versagen der Regierung öffentlich und international anzuklagen. Wir nehmen dabei kein Blatt vor den Mund. Wir schweigen nicht, denn es ist eine wichtige Prämisse nicht zu schweigen, niemals zu schweigen! Wer Missstände und Menschenrechtsverletzungen in Mexiko dokumentiert, aufdeckt und öffentlich kritisiert, gilt als Bedrohung.

Angriffe auf Menschenrechtsverteidiger:innen, Aktivist:innen und kritische Journalist:innen sind aber ein globales Problem. Wir fordern, dass sich Regierungen weltweit zusammensetzen und dem endlich einen Riegel vorschieben. Das ist zentral, um die Demokratie zu verteidigen. Im Kontakt mit Menschenrechtsverteidiger:innen und Aktivist:innen, die für Gerechtigkeit streiten, erlebe ich jeden Tag, wie wichtig und relevant unsere Arbeit ist. Wenn wir es zum Beispiel schaffen, ein Urteil zu erstreiten, den Staat in die Verantwortung zu nehmen und damit ein Stück Gerechtigkeit für die Mutter einer ermordeten Tochter herzustellen oder Schutzmaßnahmen für bedrohte Aktivist:innen zu erstreiten, wissen wir, welchen Wert unsere Arbeit hat. Ich will in einer Atmosphäre extremer Gewalt und Menschenrechtsverletzungen Samen der Hoffnung und des Friedens säen. Unsere Mission ist es, demokratische Veränderungen anzustoßen, für würdige Lebensbedingungen einzustehen und Gerechtigkeit einzufordern. Das ist eine Lebensaufgabe.

Consorcio Oaxaca is a feminist human rights organization that has been advocating for human rights and denouncing abuses since 2011. We face attacks and intimidation because of our work. However, we will not cease to document the violence against women and the severe human rights crisis in our country, both publicly and internationally. We will continue to denounce the government's failures and will not mince matters. We will not remain silent because it is of utter importance not to remain silent, never to remain silent! Those who document, expose, and publicly criticize abuses and human rights violations in Mexico are considered a threat.

Attacks on human rights defenders, activists, and critical journalists are a global problem. We demand that governments worldwide come together and finally put an end to this. This is crucial to defend democracy. In contact with human rights defenders and activists fighting for justice, I experience every day how important and relevant our work is. For example, when we manage to obtain a judgment, hold the state accountable, and thereby achieve some justice for the mother of a murdered daughter or secure protective measures for threatened activists. That's when we understand and see the value of our work. In an atmosphere of extreme violence and human rights violations, I want to sow seeds of hope and peace. Our mission is to initiate democratic changes, to stand up for dignified living conditions, and to demand justice. This is our purpose in life.

Democracy undergoing change worldwide?

» Broccoli, Brussels sprouts, spinach or lentils.
You can choose what you want to eat democratically.«
»Then, I'll prefer a sausage dictatorship. «

German populists fear a prohibition of meat dishes whenever a more plant-based diet is favored and often use the word »dictatorship« in this context.

Nachdenkliches zum 8. März

Thoughts on International Women's Day

»Really? All dictators around the world are male?«
»Maybe we should introduce a women's quota?«

»Do not worry. We only send you into quarantine.«

Gegenstände aus dem Museum der australischen Demokratie

Das Gemeinwohl

Faktenbasierte Politik

Anhörung der Öffentlichkeit beim Verkauf von öffentlichem Eigentum

Transparenz

Der Geist ministerieller Standards

Pfeifen

Unstrittig

»Wenn wir weniger testen, haben wir weniger Covid-19-Fälle.«

»Wenn du Kritiker zum Schweigen bringst, sind alle mit dir einverstanden.«

»Wenn du Wahlen verhinderst, kann man dich nicht abwählen.«

»Wenn du die Leute nicht zählst, ist die Menge RIESIG!«

VEIL OF POWER

Schleier der Macht

We appreciate your interest!
We are demolishing democracy.

Save the climate!

»We want to vote!«
»You are allowed to demonstrate. That should be enough!«

»Please let me introduce another part of our modern migration policy.«

Democracy for Myanmar

»This is not an easy virus to defeat.«

»Ein Blick in Europas dunkle Vergangenheit«
»… oder in seine Zukunft.«

Extreme Rechte

Schweden Polen Deutschland Österreich Ungarn

The Arab Spring

STOP. The European winter starts here.

CHAPPATTE

There is an online test [Wahl-O-Mat] you can take before every German election in order to find the party closest to your own political beliefs. It has already been hacked several times.

»Can't I stomp through puddles in peace for once?« – » Do I always have to help?*«

*Yes (comment by the cartoonist)

Wahl 2024

Wähle eine Kiste

»Die Wähler wollen nicht, dass Biden oder Trump ein zweites Mal antreten. Trotzdem machen sie es wieder.«

»Beide Parteien lassen dritte Parteien nicht am Rennen teilnehmen.«

»Und wenn ich mich weigere zu wählen, werde ich als unpatriotisch beschimpft.«

»Das ist Demokratie!«

»Das stimmt nicht …«

Extreme Rechte

Unruhen in Frankreich

»Do Hungary and Poland veto or have we switched their power off?«

Even though they are members of the EU, Hungary and Poland regularly veto EU-wide decisions thus blocking further progress.

Antisemitism is part of Germany!

Justizreform in Israel   Judicial Reform in Israel

Wähler und Kandidaten

Um die Wahl zu gewinnen, versprechen die Kandidaten den Wählern vieles. Dabei geht es den Kandidaten nur um Macht. Sind sie gewählt, haben sie diktatorische Züge und halten sich nicht an ihre Wahlversprechen. In der Folge leiden die Wähler.

Voters and Candidates.

In order to win the elections, candidates make many promises. However, candidates simply want to come to power. Once elected, they have dictatorial inclinations and do not fulfill their electoral promises. As a result, voters start to suffer.

Politische Debatten sind Wettkämpfe. Der Politiker mit der besten Rhetorik gewinnt.

Political debates are often like competitions, and the most eloquent politician wins.

Protestierende wissen nicht, wohin ihr Protest führt. Manchmal führen ihre Forderungen sogar zu ihrem Tod.

Protesters often don't know exactly where their protest leads them. Sometimes, these protests can even lead to their death.

»Our election observer.«

Stimmenzähler in Belarus

Counting Votes in Belarus

Wahlsieger in Sicht   Winner in Sight

»Why should I vote?«

The first column of the results shows the impact of non-voters.

Gerichtssaal

Gewissen

Nein zu Gewalt

»Diese Feministen gehören nicht zu unserer Zivilisation!«

»Wir haben Ihnen gesagt, dass Pressefreiheit unsere rote Linie ist.«

»There's no law against thinking that.«

»There's no law against saying that.«

»There's no law against voting that.«

There are no lies on the internet.

»How do you know that?«
»Why? I asked Google.«

»When I'm grown up, I want to become like you: give a shit about my children.«

OBY EZEKWESILI

Obiageli »Oby« Katryn Ezekwesili, ehemalige Präsidentschaftskandidatin Nigerias für die Wahlen 2019, ist Expertin für Wirtschaftspolitik und leitende Wirtschaftsberaterin bei der Africa Economic Development Policy Initiative (AEDPI) und Mitbegründerin der Bewegung #BringBackOurGirls in Nigeria.

Ezekwesili war Vizepräsidentin der Weltbank (Region Afrika), Ministerin für Bildung und Ministerin für Mineralien in Nigeria, Vorsitzende der Budget Monitoring and Price Intelligence Unit und Vorsitzende der Nigerian Extractive Industry Transparency Initiative (NEITI). Sie ist außerdem Gründungsdirektorin von Transparency International. Derzeit ist Ezekwesili Vorsitzende des Vorstands von Women Political Leaders (WPL) in Brüssel und unterstreicht damit ihr Engagement für die Förderung von Frauen in der Politik weltweit.

Obiageli »Oby« Katryn Ezekwesili, presidential candidate of Nigeria in the 2019 elections, is an economic policy expert and Senior Economic Advisor at the Africa Economic Development Policy Initiative (AEDPI) and co-founder of the #BringBackOurGirls movement in Nigeria.

Ezekwesili was Vice President of the World Bank (Africa Region), Minister of Education and Minister of Solid Minerals in Nigeria, Chairperson of the Budget Monitoring and Price Intelligence Unit and Chairperson of the Nigerian Extractive Industry Transparency Initiative (NEITI). She is also a founding director of Transparency International. Currently, Ezekwesili chairs the board of Women Political Leaders (WPL) in Brussels, emphasizing her commitment to advancing women in politics globally.

Bürgerinnen und Bürger weltweit und insbesondere auf dem afrikanischen Kontinent sind es leid, dass sich Wahlzyklen einfach wiederholen. Sie wollen Wahlen, die eine gute Regierungsführung und die Vorteile eines demokratischen Prozesses hervorbringen.

Demokratie geht mit politischer Freiheit einher. Mit politischer Freiheit geht Rechtsstaatlichkeit einher, die der Grundstein für wirtschaftliche Freiheit ist. Es ist die wirtschaftliche Freiheit, die zur Verbreitung von Ideen, Innovationen und Kreativität führt. Deshalb müssen wir starke Institutionen aufbauen und Transparenz und Rechenschaftspflicht auf allen Ebenen der Regierung fördern. Dies wird ein Umfeld schaffen, das Investitionen des Privatsektors, die Schaffung von Arbeitsplätzen und Wirtschaftswachstum ermöglicht.

Durch die Einstufung von Menschenrechtsverletzungen als internationales Verbrechen würde sich die Welt von ihrer derzeitigen unheilvollen Rolle als duldende Zuschauerin oder ungewollt aktive Teilnehmerin an den eklatanten Verstößen von Staaten befreien, die nicht bereit sind, die Grundsätze der bürgerlichen, politischen, wirtschaftlichen und sozialen Rechte ihrer Bürger:innen zu beachten oder durchzusetzen.

Die Vorstellung, weltweit Frieden haben zu können, ohne sich um die Verubung dieser abscheulichen Taten zu kümmern, ist moralisch verwerflich. Unbestreitbar ist hingegen, dass Gerechtigkeit und Rechtsstaatlichkeit die Grundlagen für Frieden und Sicherheit sind.

Citizens worldwide and especially on the African continent are tired of simply repeating electoral cycles. They want elections that lead to good governance and the benefits of democratic processes.

Democracy comes along with political freedom. And with political freedom comes the rule of law, the cornerstone of economic freedom. And it is economic freedom that leads to the proliferation of ideas, innovations, and creativity.

Therefore, we need to build strong institutions and promote transparency and accountability on all government levels. This will lead to an environment that enables private sector investments, job creation, and economic growth.

By classifying human rights violations as an international crime, the world would free itself from its current ominous role either as an acquiescing spectator or unintended active participant in the flagrant infringements committed by states. States which are either unwilling to observe or enforce the principles of their citizens' civil, political, economic, and social rights.

The idea that we can have global peace while paying no attention to the perpetration of these heinous acts is morally repugnant. There is no gainsaying the fact that justice and the rule of law are the foundations for peace and security.

Afrikanische Junta

»Was ist das?«
»Ein Sprengsatz?«
»Ich sag's euch gleich, das rühr ich nicht an …«

African Junta

»What's that?«
»An explosive device?«
»Let me tell you straight away that I'm not touching it …«

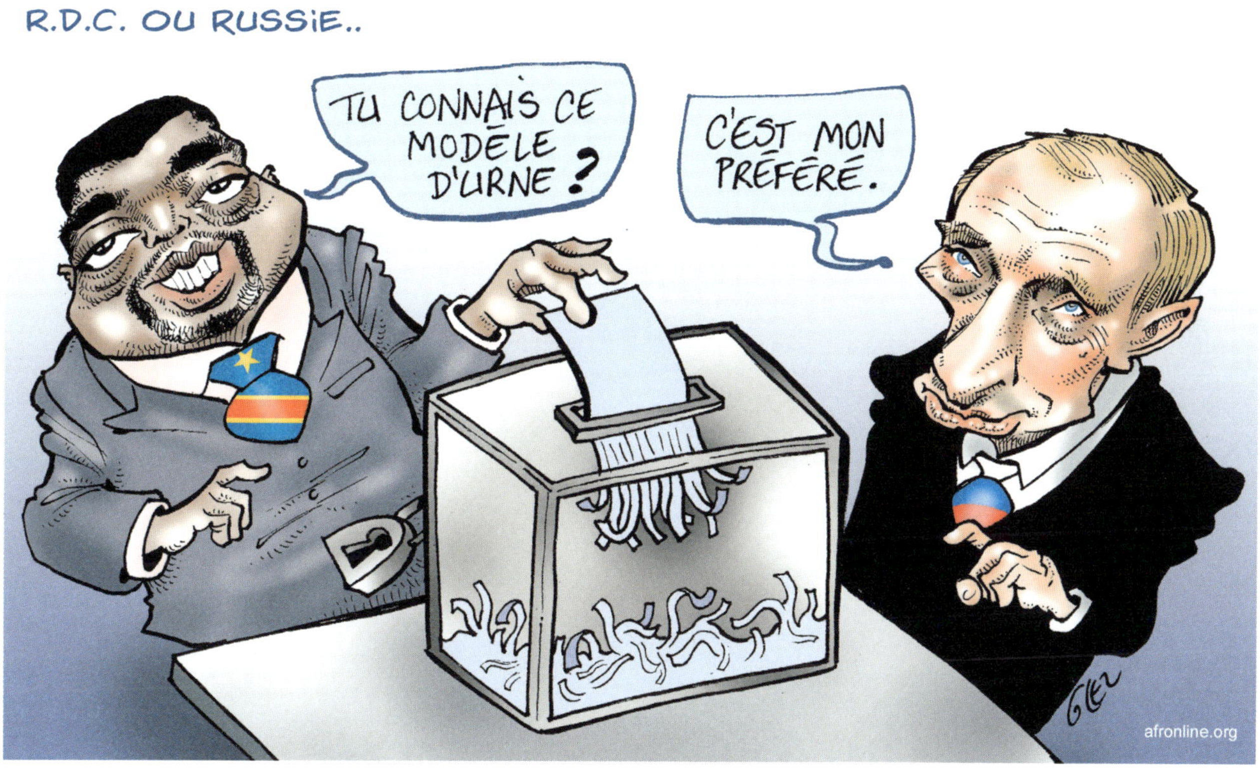

Demokratische Republik Kongo oder Russland

»Kennst du dieses Urnen-Modell?«
»Das mag ich am liebsten.«

DRC or Russia

»Have you never seen that type of ballot box?«
»That's the one I like the most.«

Korrupte Wahlen Corrupt Elections

Ruhe

Zusammenleben

Frieden

Einheit

Respekt

Silence

Social Coexistence

Peace

Unity

Respect

New Etiquette

»I am honored by your comparison to the Fuehrer.«

»Am I not allowed anymore to say that no one is allowed anymore to say anything?«

Of course, we care for democratic values, norms & tradition and want to see them empowered ...in Afghanistan!

Natürlich sind uns demokratische Werte, Normen und Traditionen wichtig und wir wollen, dass sie gestärkt werden … in Afghanistan!

NEWS
24X7
©MANJUL.

Lecturing democratic values to world leaders is fun. Whenever I try it in my own country, people start laughing

Vor Weltmarktführern über demokratische Werte zu sprechen macht Spaß. Immer, wenn ich das in meinem eigenen Land versuche, fangen die Leute an zu lachen.

»Unlike me, you can choose! For example, the coffee you'll buy!«

»Statistically speaking, I will live a lot longer on this earth …
So, why can't I have a say …?!«

Selbsthilfegruppe für Diktatoren

Support Group for Dictators

»I strongly discourage you from doing that!
Education only causes trouble!«

»I am not a racist. I couldn't stand foreigners way before the refugee crisis.«

»I must get rid of coal heating and install a heat pump, use separated cauldrons for men and women, and non-binary people. And what do I do with Wagenknecht? Put her with Hitler or Stalin? And soon Putin will come too … I can't work like this.«

Sahra Wagenknecht is a former politician of Germany's left-wing party »Die Linke« who increasingly shows populist tendencies and intends to start her own political party.

«Unity and justice and freedom …?«
»I've heard that somewhere … is it from ›Game of Thrones‹?«

The German national anthem starts with »Einigkeit und Recht und Freiheit«.

ALL YOU NEED IS LAW

»... and let it look like a state under the rule of law!«
»Aye-aye, sir!«

Die amerikanische Finsternis

MIKOŁAJ PIETRZAK

Mikołaj Pietrzak, Absolvent der Rechtswissenschaften an der Universität Warschau und Dekan des Warschauer Anwaltsgremiums, ist Mitglied des Verwaltungsrats des UN-Fonds für Opfer der Folter. Als Mitglied internationaler juristischer Organisationen ist er auf Strafrecht, Menschenrechte und Lustrationsverfahren spezialisiert.

Mikołaj Pietrzak, a University of Warsaw law graduate, is the Dean of the Warsaw Bar Council and an UN-appointed member of the Board of Trustees for the UN Voluntary Fund for Victims of Torture. As a member of international legal organizations, he specializes in criminal law, human rights, and lustration proceedings.

Die Unabhängigkeit der polnischen Anwaltskammern und die Autonomie der Disziplinarverfahren der Anwälte wurden in der Vergangenheit ständig infrage gestellt. Wir beobachteten eine ständige Zunahme von Verletzungen des Anwaltsgeheimnisses durch staatliche Behörden. Diese Bedrohung war zweifellos im Zunehmen begriffen und erforderte äußerste Wachsamkeit, und zwar nicht nur von Seiten der Anwaltschaft, sondern auch von Seiten der Zivilgesellschaft.

Die Rechtsstaatlichkeit ist ein Wert, der den Kern unseres Berufs darstellt. Als Anwälte haben wir die Aufgabe, Rechte und Freiheiten zu schützen. Es kann keinen Schutz der Rechte und Freiheiten in einem Staat geben, in dem politische Willkür Vorrang vor dem Recht hat. Die Rechtsstaatlichkeit steht im Mittelpunkt unserer beruflichen Wertegrundlage und es ist unsere ethische Pflicht, sie zu verteidigen, wenn sie bedroht ist.

Wir sind ein Beispiel dafür, wie wichtig es für Anwälte ist, wachsam zu bleiben und auf die ersten Anzeichen von demokratischen Rückschritten und Verletzungen grundlegender Verfassungsprinzipien zu reagieren. Letztendlich sind wir alle Menschenrechtsanwälte und teilen eine gemeinsame Reihe von rechtlichen Werten, die auf der Rechtsstaatlichkeit beruhen und die wir jeden Tag durch unsere zivilgesellschaftliche Beteiligung und durch demokratische Entscheidungen bei Wahlen schützen müssen.

The independence of the Polish bar associations and the autonomy of advocates' disciplinary proceedings were constantly challenged in the past. We observed increasing violations of attorney-client privilege by state authorities. This threat was certainly on the rise and it required extreme vigilance, not only by our legal community, but also by civil society.

The rule of law as a value is the very core of our profession. As lawyers, it is our duty to protect rights and freedoms. And there can be no protection of the rights and freedoms in a state where arbitrary political power takes priority over the law. The rule of law is at the centre of our profession's values and, when threatened, it is our ethical duty to come to its defense.

We are an example for how critical it is for lawyers to remain vigilant, to react to the first signs of a democratic setback and to violations of basic constitutional principles. Ultimately, we are all human rights lawyers. And we share a common set of legal values based on the rule of law which we need to protect every day by participating in civil society and making democratic choices at elections.

Ab jetzt keine Hassreden mehr!!!

No hate speech from now on!!!

Polnischer Sisyphos Polish Sisyphus

ARKADIUSZ KRUPA, POLEN/POLAND

»Und was ist mit den allgemeingültigen Menschenrechten?«
»Sie werden weitgehend missachtet.«

»And what about universal human rights?«
»They are widely ignored.«

Social Distancing
Members of AfD refrain from shaking hands

AfD (Alternative für Deutschland/Alternative for Germany) is the biggest right-wing political party in Germany. Some of its members have an extreme right-wing background.

Wake up!

»Mama, what are we going to do on Mondays once the lies about Corona are in the past?«
»Don't worry. For sure, there will be refugees threatening our democracy.«

Monday demonstrations that were first introduced in the GDR in 1989 are nowadays instrumentalized by right-wing populists.

»Mama, if that's Europe, why do we want to go there?«

Broken Traffic Lights.

»It only ever shows yellow.«

The German government elected in 2021 consists of three parties: SPD (red logo), Die Grünen (green logo), and FDP (blue and yellow logo). Their coalition is called »Die Ampel« by the media.

»Last Generation? Next door, henchman.«
»Thank you and please excuse the disturbance …«

HKNKRZ stands for swastika.

Angriff auf das Kapitol

United States Capitol Attack

Rechtsstaat Iran

Iran: a constitutional state

Rude awakening after AfD's lavish electoral party.
»Who's the culprit?!?«

AfD (Alternative für Deutschland/Alternative for Germany) is the biggest right-wing political party in Germany. Some of its members have an extreme right-wing background.

»We must crack down on them! Those demonstrators are armed to the teeth!«
»Using what?«
»Values!«

LAND SCHULZ

Flug in die Freiheit Flight to Freedom

Pressefreiheit Freedom of Press

Zensur von Cartoonist:innen

Censorship of Cartoonists

We have only singled you out to tell you that we do not apply any racial profiling.

Democracy's future?

Class representative elections

»I'll stage a coup against you, you tool!«

The Brown Armchair

»In the past, the talk show was named after its host. But they needed a new name because they always invited a Nazi.«

»I would like to thank all protest voters for our wonderful election results. As a first act, we will abolish the right to vote!«

»I'm afraid that the people I vote will form the government.«

Der Morgen danach

The Morning After

»I didn't do it!«

»And what's so great about these election results?«
»It could have been way worse.«

»The ruling from Luxembourg is ridiculous!
We aren't states under the rule of law?!
What are we then?!!«
»Left-wing states?«

This is a wordplay in German. »Rechts« can mean both »right-wing« and »under the rule of law«.

EU Parliament

European elections

»Well, it is very generous to be invited to the demolition.«

You can see a tiny flag with the logo of »Alternative für Deutschland«, the biggest German right-wing party.

The constitutional state of Germany

»We are convinced that we can guarantee your right to wear a kippa in public.
Right now, we are only discussing if we can also guarantee your safety.«

»Oh! Sie sagen Bescheid, wenn ich störe! «

NEIN!

CRS: Kasernierter Verband der Police Nationale.

»Oh! Please let me know if I'm interrupting!«

NO!

CRS: General Reserve of the French National Police.

Abzug aus Afghanistan

»Jungs! Das müsst ihr sehen!
Sie haben uns einen Riesenvorrat
an Demokratie dagelassen!«

Withdrawal from Afghanistan

»Guys! You have to see that!
They have left us a huge
supply of democracy!«

Wählen Sie!

»Das hier haben wir noch nicht probiert.«

Vote!

»We haven't tried this one yet.«

HOMEIRA QADERI

Die 1980 in Kabul geborene Homeira Qaderi studierte und arbeitete als Professorin in Iran. Als Frauenrechtlerin beriet sie das afghanische Ministerium für Arbeit und Soziales. Im August 2021 gehörte sie zu den letzten, die Afghanistan verließen. Heute lebt und arbeitet sie als Aktivistin, Autorin und Professorin in den USA.

Born in Kabul in 1980, Homeira Qaderi studied and worked as a professor in Iran. As a women's rights advocate, she advised the Afghan Ministry of Labor and Social Affairs. In August 2021, she was among the last to leave Afghanistan. Today, she lives and works as an activist, author, and professor in the USA.

Die afghanischen Frauen, die während der demokratischen Entwicklung zwischen 2001 und 2021 ein gewisses Maß an Bürgerrechten und Freiheiten erlangt hatten, gehen heute auf die Straße, wenn auch nur in geringer Zahl, da sie der Gefahr ausgesetzt sind, von den Taliban ausgepeitscht, gefoltert, inhaftiert oder noch schlimmer behandelt zu werden. Die Verhängung noch strengerer Beschränkungen für Frauen durch die Taliban ist beunruhigend und die Preisgabe der Angelegenheiten der Frauen durch die afghanischen Männer erinnert uns daran, dass die Verteidigung der Menschenrechte in Afghanistan immer noch die Hilfe der internationalen Gemeinschaft benötigt.

Insbesondere ein kultureller Wandel erfordert gut finanzierte Programme, ehrgeizige Pädagog:innen und engagierte politische Spitzen, die an die Gleichstellung der Geschlechter glauben. Die Frauen haben sich selbst und die Kämpfe, die sie führen müssen, um ihren rechtmäßigen Platz in der Gesellschaft wiederzuerlangen, erkannt. Eine Kunst, die diesen Werten wirklich verpflichtet ist, könnte der afghanischen Bevölkerung das Alphabet der Freiheit beibringen.

Kunst – mit all ihren ermächtigenden Fähigkeiten in den Bereichen Belletristik, Poesie, Kino, Theater, Malerei, Musik oder Fotografie – könnte zur Förderung einer gerechteren sozialen Dynamik beitragen und positive Veränderungen bei Meinungen, Überzeugungen, Werten und Normen bewirken. Um solche Entwicklungen zu erreichen, braucht es Zeit und Mühe, einen Plan und ein Budget, aber vor allem einen echten Glauben an die Möglichkeit eines sozialen Wandels.

Afghan women achieved a modicum of civil rights and liberties during the democratic development from 2001 to 2021. Nowadays they have taken to the streets, albeit in small numbers due to the risk of being lashed, tortured, and detained by the Taliban, or being treated even worse. The imposition of increasingly severe restrictions on women in Afghanistan is alarming. And the abandonment of the women's cause by Afghan men reminds us that the defense of human rights in Afghanistan still needs help from the international community.

Cultural change requires well-funded programs, ambitious educators, and committed political leaders who believe in gender equality. Women have come to understand themselves and the battles they need to fight to regain their rightful place in society. An art that is truly committed to such values could teach Afghan people the alphabet of freedom.

Art – with its empowering capacity in the areas of fiction writing, poetry, cinema, theatre, painting, music, or photography – could contribute to the promotion of more equitable social dynamics and prompt positive changes in opinions, beliefs, values, and norms. Achieving such developments takes time and effort. And it requires a plan as well as a budget. But above all, it calls for a genuine belief in the possibility of social change.

Abzug der USA aus Afghanistan Withdrawal of US Troops from Afghanistan

Meinungsfreiheit auf der Welt   Free Speech around the World

Keine Pressefreiheit No Freedom of Press

Söder confronts Aiwanger

»Jokes about Jews? Nazi salute? I've got no idea. As a boy, I just wanted no space between the right wall and myself! Not even a blotter!«

Aiwanger, a Bavarian politician, probably wrote an antisemitic pamphlet in his youth. When the news came out in 2023, the governor of Bavaria Markus Söder confronted him but took no consequences for their coalition in Bavaria.

Zu den Waffen, Reichsbürger!

To Arms, Citizens of the Reich!

I do not acknowledge the German state except for the German Shooting Federation and its gun licences!

Ex-Verfassungsschutzchef Maaßen zum Hanaumassaker

Former Head of the Protection for the Constitution on the massacre in Hanau

»What about the constant accusation of right-wing terror?
Otto Schily and I would first investigate the Turkish milieu for the next 10 years!«

On February 19th, 2020 nine immigrants were shot in Hanau, Germany. The Federal Criminal Police Office in Germany classified the attack as an extreme right-wing and racist act.

Private Circle

Last Generation

»If I am part of a criminal organization, at least I am wearing a robe!«

»In jeder Gesellschaft, egal in welchem politischen System, gibt es zwei Arten von Leuten.
Die einen sind glücklich, wenn einer aus ihrer Mitte Rechte und Sicherheit einbüßt.
Und die anderen, die der Meinung sind, dass das nicht nur unfair, sondern auch eine Gefahr für die Demokratie an sich darstellt.«

»Also kommt es nur darauf an, was für ein Typ Mensch man sein möchte.«

»Genau das, weiser Eber.«

DEMOCRACY
TARTAROTTI

FREEDOM CARTOONISTS FOUNDATION

Für die Freedom Cartoonist Foundation mit Sitz in Genf sind Cartoons ein zentraler Bestandteil des öffentlichen Diskurses. Die Stiftung steht für Pressefreiheit und ist der Überzeugung, dass politischen Cartoons dabei eine entscheidende Rolle zukommt. Sich für freie Meinungsäußerung durch Dialog einzusetzen steht im Zentrum ihrer Mission.

In einem Rhythmus von zwei Jahren verleiht die Freedom Cartoonist Foundation seit 2012 gemeinsam mit der Stadt Genf den internationalen Cartoonpreis »The Kofi Annan Courage in Cartooning Award«, der nach dem verstorbenen Ehrenvorsitzenden der Stiftung benannt wurde. Parallel zu diesem Preis wird rund um den Genfer See eine Cartoon-Ausstellung veranstaltet.

Die Stiftung, deren Vorsitz der Cartoonist Patrick Chappatte und die ehemalige UN-Sprecherin Marie Heuzé innehaben, verwaltet darüber hinaus einen Fonds zur Unterstützung bedrohter Cartoonist:innen und organisiert pädagogische Projekte zur Förderung der Kreativität, der Toleranz und eines besseren Verständnisses der Menschenrechte.

Based in Geneva, Switzerland, the Freedom Cartoonists Foundation supports professional editorial cartooning as an essential part of public debate and stands for a free press as a pillar of democracy. It is the Foundation's belief that political cartoons are a vital element of such a free press. The defence of freedom of speech through dialogue is the Foundation's mission.

Since 2012 the Foundation and the City of Geneva have been presenting »The Kofi Annan Courage in Cartooning Award«, their biennial international editorial cartoon award which was named after the foundation's late honorary chairman. In parallel to the award, a cartoon exhibition takes place on the shores of Lake Geneva.

The Foundation which is chaired by cartoonist Patrick Chappatte and former UN spokesperson Marie Heuzé also manages a support fund for threatened editorial cartoonists and organizes educational projects aimed at fostering creativity, tolerance, and a better understanding of human rights.

www.freedomcartoonists.com

Freedom Cartoonists
DESSINS POUR LA LIBERTÉ

CARTOONING FOR PEACE

Cartooning for Peace wurde 2006 durch die Initiative des früheren Generalsekretärs der Vereinten Nationen Kofi Annan und des Cartoonisten Plantu gegründet. Über die universelle Sprache der Cartoons setzen sich die Mitglieder des internationalen Netzwerks für Meinungsfreiheit, Menschenrechte und gegenseitigen Respekt unabhängig von Herkunft und Glauben ein. Den Vorsitz der gemeinnützigen Organisation nach französischem Recht hat derzeit der französische Cartoonist Kak inne.

Förderung von Cartoons

Die Organisation sieht Cartoons als Informationsquelle und Mittel für den öffentlichen demokratischen Diskurs an. Neben Ausstellungen, Veröffentlichungen und der regelmäßigen Zusammenarbeit mit den Medien werden auch Veranstaltungen organisiert, bei denen Cartoonist:innen und die Öffentlichkeit zusammenkommen.

Bildung mithilfe von Cartoons

Bildung mithilfe von Cartoons und der Unterricht in freier Meinungsäußerung stehen im Zentrum der Arbeit. Die Organisation engagiert sich in Schulen, im außerschulischen Bereich und in Gefängnissen und sensibilisiert über Humor für große gesellschaftliche Probleme.

Schutz von Cartoonist:innen

Als eine Hauptmission macht die Organisation die Öffentlichkeit und Institutionen auf Angriffe auf die Freiheit von Cartoonist:innen aufmerksam, die unter erschwerten Umständen arbeiten, und bietet bei Bedarf Unterstützung an.

Created in 2006 on the initiative of the former Secretary General of the United Nations Kofi Annan and the cartoonist Plantu, Cartooning for Peace is an international network of cartoonists committed to promoting freedom of expression, human rights, and mutual respect among people of different cultural backgrounds and beliefs through the universal language of cartoons. Registered as an organisation of general interest under French law, it is currently chaired by the French cartoonist Kak.

Promoting Press Cartoons

The organisation promotes press cartoons as a tool for information and democratic debate among the general public. Besides exhibitions, publications, and regular collaborations with the media, it also organises events where cartoonists and the general public can meet.

Educating Through Press Cartoons

Education through press cartoons and education in freedom of expression are at the heart of the organisation's approach. It regularly intervenes in schools, out-of-school contexts, and prisons. Through humor, Cartooning for Peace raises awareness of major social problems.

Defending Cartoonists

As one of its main missions, the organisation alerts the general public and institutions on attacks on the freedom of cartoonists who work in difficult contexts and provides support where needed.

www.cartooningforpeace.org

CARTOONISTEN/CARTOONISTS

Amorim, Brasilien/Brazil

Carlos Alberto da Costa AMORIM, geb. 1964 in Rio de Janeiro, Brasilien. Preisgekrönter Comic- und Cartoonzeichner, Illustrator und Autor. Veröffentlicht in zahlreichen brasilianischen Zeitungen und Zeitschriften, illustriert Kinderbücher und unterrichtet seit 1994 Comics und Karikaturen (Rio de Janeiro-Brasilien).

Carlos Alberto da Costa AMORIM, born 1964 in Rio de Janeiro, Brazil. Award-winning comic and cartoon artist, illustrator and author. Published in numerous Brazilian newspapers and magazines, illustrates children's books and has been teaching comics and cartoons since 1994 (Rio de Janeiro-Brazil).

Frank Bahr, Deutschland/Germany

1969 in Stuttgart, Süddeutschland, geboren, lebt an und auf der Ostsee und arbeitet als freier Maler und Cartoonist.

Born in 1969 in Stuttgart, southern Germany, lives on and around the Baltic Sea and works as a freelance painter and cartoonist. www.frank-bahr.net

Harm Bengen, Deutschland/Germany

Lebt in Norden, Ostfriesland, wo er 1955 geboren wurde, als freier Cartoonist und Comiczeichner. Veröffentlicht in diversen Zeitschriften und Zeitungen.

Lives in Arle, East Frisia as a freelance cartoonist and comic artist, where he was born in 1955. Published in various magazines and newspapers. www.harm-bengen.de

Camille Besse, Frankreich/France

Camille Besse, 1983 geboren, wuchs in Paris auf. Nach einem siebenjährigen Studium wurde sie Graphic Designer und startete ihre Karriere als Cartoonistin bei *Charlie Hebdo*. Zurzeit zeichnet sie für ca. zehn Zeitungen und Zeitschriften, u.a. *Causette, Marianne, L'Humanité, Le Pélerin*. Außerdem arbeitet sie als Comiczeichnerin und animiert TV-Trickfilme.

Camille Besse, born in 1983, grew up in Paris. After studying for seven years, she became a graphic designer and began her career as a cartoonist at *Charlie Hebdo*. She currently draws for around ten newspapers and magazines, including *Causette, Marianne, L'Humanité and Le Pélerin.* She also works as a comic artist and animates TV cartoons. www.instagram.com/bessedessins

Bettina Bexte, Deutschland/Germany

Geboren 1965, lebt in Bremen und ist seit dem Kunststudium als freie Illustratorin und Cartoonistin tätig. Ihre Arbeiten erscheinen in zahlreichen Zeitschriften, 2023 gewann sie den 1. Platz des *Deutschen Karikaturenpreises.*

Born in 1965, lives in Bremen and has worked as a freelance illustrator and cartoonist since studying art. Her work has appeared in numerous magazines and in 2023 she won first place in the *German Caricature Prize*. www.bettina-bexte.de

BURKH, Deutschland/Germany

1952 in Mölln geboren, lebt in Köln. Der vielfach preisgekrönte Zeichner (zuletzt 2023 der Publikumspreis des Deutschen Karikaturenpreises), lange Jahre als Dozent für Karikatur und Satire in Münster tätig, ist seit 1980 freier Cartoonist und Karikaturist, zeichnete oder zeichnet für zahlreiche Buchverlage, Zeitungen und Zeitschriften wie *taz, Eulenspiegel, Kicker* und die deutsche Ausgabe von *Charlie Hebdo*.

Born in Mölln in 1952; lives in Cologne. The multiple award-winning illustrator (most recently the Audience Award of the German Caricature Prize in 2023), who worked for many years as a lecturer in caricature and satire in Münster, has been a freelance cartoonist and caricaturist since 1980, for numerous book publishers, newspapers and magazines such as *taz, Eulenspiegel, Kicker* and the German edition of *Charlie Hebdo*. www.burkh.com

Chapatte, Schweiz/Switzerland

Patrick Chappatte wurde 1967 in Karachi, Pakistan, als Sohn eines Schweizer Vaters und einer libanesischen Mutter geboren. Er ist ein politischer Karikaturist und Comic-Reporter, der für internationale Medien wie *Der Spiegel* und *The Boston Globe* arbeitet. 20 Jahre lang war er redaktioneller Karikaturist der New York Times. Zusammen mit Plantu gründete er die Schweizer Stiftung *Cartooning for Peace*, die 2020 in *Freedom Cartoonists* umbenannt wurde. Heute ist er Vorsitzender der Stiftung, die ihren Sitz in Genf hat, wo er auch lebt und arbeitet.

Patrick Chappatte was born in 1967 in Karachi, Pakistan, to a Swiss father and a Lebanese mother. He is a political cartoonist and comics reporter; he works for the international media such as *Der Spiegel* and *The Boston Globe*. For 20 years, he was the editorial cartoonist of The New York Times. Together with Plantu, he co-founded the Swiss foundation *Cartooning for Peace*, renamed *Freedom Cartoonists* in 2020. He now chairs the Foundation based in Geneva where he lives and works. www.globecartoon.com

Darío Castillejos, Mexiko/Mexico

1974 in der mexikanischen Stadt Oaxaca geboren, arbeitete er für die Zeitungen El imparcial de Oaxaca, El Chamuco und die Zeitschriften Courrier International und Foreign Affairs Latinoamérica sowie für Agenturen. Derzeit ist er Präsident des *CartonClub*, des lateinamerikanischen Karikaturenclubs. Seine Karikaturen wurden mit zahlreichen Preisen ausgezeichnet, darunter dreimal mit dem *Nationalen Journalistenpreis* in Mexiko und dem *World Press Cartoon* in Portugal.

Born in 1974 in Oaxaca in Mexico, he has collaborated for the newspapers *El imparcial de Oaxaca, El Chamuco* and the magazines *Courrier International* and *Foreign Affairs Latinoamérica,* as well as for agencies. He is currently president of *CartonClub*, the Latin American caricature club. His cartoons have won numerous awards, including the *National Journalism Award* in Mexico three times and the *World Press Cartoon* in Portugal.

Doaa Eladl, Ägypten/Egypt

1979 geboren, lebt und arbeitet als Karikaturistin und Illustratorin in Kairo. Studierte Kunstwissenschaften an der Universität Alexandria, seit 2007 erscheinen ihre Cartoons in verschiedensten Zeitungen und Magazinen, u.a. *al-Dustour, Rose-al-Yusuf* und *Sabah El Kheir*, aktuell in der unabhängigen ägyptischen Tageszeitung *al-Masry al-Youm*. Ihre politischen und gesellschaftskritischen Zeichnungen, auch zur Rolle der Frau, lösten bereits mehrfach heftige Debatten in Ägypten aus.

Born in 1979; lives and works as a cartoonist and illustrator in Cairo. She studied art at Alexandria University and since 2007 her cartoons have appeared in various newspapers and magazines, including *al-Dustour, Rose-al-Yusuf* and *Sabah El Kheir*. Her work is currently published in the independent Egyptian daily newspaper *al-Masry al-Youm*. Her political and socially critical drawings, including on the role of women, have repeatedly triggered heated debates in Egypt. www.instagram.com/doaa.eladl.cartoon

Rod Emmerson, Neuseeland/Newzealand

Geboren 1955 in Australien, lebt heute in Neuseeland. Mehrfach preisgekrönter politischer Karikaturist und Künstler. Seit 2003 ist er Karikaturist für den *New Zealand Herald*, zuvor arbeitete er für *APN News & Media* in Queensland, Australien. Seine Arbeiten wurden von der *New York Times Syndicate* und *Associated Press* veröffentlicht.

Born in Australia in 1955, he now lives in New Zealand. Multi-award winning political cartoonist and artist. Editorial Cartoonist for the *New Zealand Herald* since 2003; he previously worked for *APN News & Media* in Queensland, Australia. His work has been published by the *New York Times Syndicate* and *Associated Press*. www.instagram.com/rodemmerson

Tim Oliver Feicke, Deutschland/Germany

Geb. 1970, lebt und zeichnet in Hamburg und ist im Hauptberuf Richter. Er ist Mitglied im Cartoonkollektiv *Hamburger Strich* und veröffentlicht in Zeitschriften und Zeitungen.

Born in 1970; lives and draws in Hamburg and is a judge by profession. He is a member of the *Hamburger Strich* cartoon collective and publishes in magazines and newspapers. www.feickecartoons.de

Fares Garabet, Syrien/Syria

Geboren 1963 in Damaskus, studierte er in Damaskus, Rom und Kairo Graphik Design und Animation. Seit 1993 war er Professor, 2006 bis 2015 Dekan der IUST an der Internationalen Universität Damaskus, und zeichnete für die Zeitungen *Alwatan* und *Alraya* in Syrien. 2016 floh er nach Deutschland, wo er heute in Dresden lebt. Er veröffentlicht in der *Süddeutschen Zeitung* und *Almajalla* in London.

Born in Damascus in 1963, he studied graphic design and animation in Damascus, Rome and Cairo. He has been a professor since 1993 and was Dean of the IUST at the International University of Damascus from 2006 to 2015 drawing for the newspapers *Alwatan* and *Alraya* in Syria. In 2016, he fled to Germany where he now lives in Dresden. His work is published in the *Süddeutsche Zeitung* and *Almajalla* in London.

Damien Glez, Burkina Faso

Damien Glez, geboren 1967, ist ein französisch-burkinischer Pressezeichner, Kolumnist, Texter, Lehrer, Drehbuchautor für Fernsehserien und Autor des Comicstrips »Divine comedy«. 25 Jahre lang war er stellvertretender Herausgeber der satirischen Wochenzeitung *Journal du Jeudi*. Seine Zeichnungen wurden vielfach ausgezeichnet und in mehreren Zeitschriften wie *Rolling Stone, The Africa report, World policy Journal* veröffentlicht.

Damien Glez, born in 1967, is a French-Burkinese press illustrator, columnist, copywriter, teacher, scriptwriter for television series and author of the comic strip »Divine comedy«. For 25 years, he was deputy editor of the satirical weekly *Journal du Jeudi*. His drawings have won many awards and have been published in several magazines such as *Rolling Stone, The Africa report, World policy Journal*. www.glez.org

Katharina Greve, Deutschland/Germany

1972 in Hamburg geboren, studierte in Berlin, wo sie noch heute lebt, Architektur. Ihre preisgekrönten Cartoons werden in Zeitungen und Magazinen (*Titanic, Das Magazin, neues deutschland, Süddeutsche Zeitung* u.a.) veröffentlicht.

Born in Hamburg in 1972, she studied architecture in Berlin where she still lives today. Her award-winning cartoons are published in newspapers and magazines (*Titanic, Das Magazin, neues deutschland, Süddeutsche Zeitung* and others). www.katharinagreve.de

Markus Grolik, Deutschland/Germany

1965 in München geboren, wo er noch heute lebt. Seit 1995 als freier Zeichner und Autor tätig für diverse Verlage und Agenturen. Veröffentlicht regelmäßig im *Nebelspalter, Eulenspiegel, SZ, Südkurier, gmx* u.a.

Born in Munich in 1965 where he still lives today. He has been working as a freelance illustrator and author for various publishers and agencies since 1995. Published regularly in *Nebelspalter, Eulenspiegel, SZ, Südkurier, gmx* and others. www.markus-grolik.de

Teresa Habild, Deutschland/Germany

1979 in München geboren, Studium der Visuellen Kommunikation in Offenbach am Main. Lebt als freie Cartoonistin und Illustratorin in Trier. Veröffentlichung in zahlreichen Medien, u.a. *Eulenspiegel, Titanic, Süddeutsche Zeitung*.

Born in Munich in 1979; she studied visual communication in Offenbach am Main and lives as a freelance cartoonist and illustrator in Trier. Published in numerous media including *Eulenspiegel, Titanic, Süddeutsche Zeitung*. www.h-bild.de

Osama Hajjaj, Jordanien/Jordan

Geboren 1973, arbeitet für mehrere jordanische Tageszeitungen und *Alquds alarabi* in London. Er veröffentlicht seine Karikaturen auch in der französischen Zeitung *Le Monde*. Er ist in seinem Land und in der gesamten arabischen Welt sehr bekannt. Er arbeitet auch für europäische und internationale Websites wie *CagleCartoons* und *CartoonMovement*. Er ist Mitglied der *Jordanischen Vereinigung der Pressekarikaturisten,* hat mehrere internationale Preise gewonnen und mehrere Ausstellungen organisiert.

Born in 1973; works for several Jordanian daily newspapers and *Alquds alarabi* in London. He also publishes his cartoons in the French newspaper *Le Monde*. He is very well known in his country and throughout the Arab world. He also works for European and international websites such as *CagleCartoons* and *CartoonMovement*. He is a member of the *Jordanian Press Cartoonists Association*, won several international awards, and organized several exhibitions. www.osama-hajjaj.com

Ruth Hebler, Deutschland/Germany

Geboren 1973, lebt in Köln. Sie ist Autodidaktin. Ihre Cartoons sind in Zeitschriften, Büchern, Kalendern und Ausstellungen zu sehen, 2021 wurde sie mit dem zweiten und 2023 mit dem dritten Platz des *Deutschen Cartoonpreises* ausgezeichnet.

Born in 1973; lives in Cologne. She is self-taught. Her cartoons can be found in magazines, books, calendars and exhibitions. In 2021, she was awarded second and in 2023 third place of *German Cartoon Prize*. www.ruthhebler.de

Michael Holtschulte, Deutschland/Germany

1979 geb., lebt und arbeitet als Cartoonist und Illustrator in Essen. Zeichnet für zahlreiche Zeitungen und Magazine und betreibt den Cartoon-Podcast *Zwei Stricher packen aus* zusammen mit Oli Hilbring.

Born in 1979; lives and works as a cartoonist and illustrator in Essen. He draws for numerous newspapers and magazines and runs the cartoon podcast *Zwei Stricher packen aus* together with Oli Hilbring. www.totaberlustig.de

Björn Karnebogen, Deutschland/Germany

Er verbindet Design und Humor in Text und Bild. 2021 gewann der den *Deutschen Cartoonpreis*.

He combines design and humor in text and images. He won the *German Cartoon Prize* in 2021 www.instagram.com/adkarnebogen

Musa Kart, Türkei/Turkey

Geboren 1954 in Konya, arbeitete 25 Jahre für Cumhuriyet, die älteste oppositionelle Zeitung der Türkei. Er war der erste Karikaturist, der nach dem Putschversuch in der Türkei verhaftet wurde, weil er Terrororganisationen unterstützt haben soll. Er verbrachte 14 Monate im Gefängnis. Im Jahr 2020 entschied der Europäische Gerichtshof für Menschenrechte, dass die Türkei »das Recht auf freie Meinungsäußerung und das Recht auf persönliche Freiheit und Sicherheit« verletzt hat und verurteilte die Türkei zur Zahlung einer Entschädigung an Musa Kart und die anderen Journalisten in demselben Fall, der als »Cumhuriyet-Prozess« bekannt ist. Das Verfahren in der Türkei ist jedoch noch nicht abgeschlossen, weiterhin besteht sein internationales Reiseverbot. Zusätzlich zu zahlreichen Auszeichnungen erhielt er 2005 den *CRNI Courage in Editorial Cartooning Award*, 2006 den *Pressefreiheitspreis des türkischen Journalistenverbandes* und 2018 den *Kofi Annan Courage in Cartooning Award*. Er lebt in Istanbul und arbeitet weiterhin an Zeichentrickfilmen.

Born in Konya in 1954, he worked for *Cumhuriyet*, Turkey's oldest opposition newspaper, for 25 years. He was the first cartoonist to be arrested after the attempted coup in Turkey for allegedly supporting terrorist organizations. He spent 14 months in prison. In 2020, the European Court of Human Rights ruled that Turkey had violated »the right to freedom of expression and the right to personal liberty and security« and ordered Turkey to pay compensation to Musa Kart and the other journalists in the case known as the »Cumhuriyet trial«. However, the proceedings in Turkey are still ongoing and he is still banned from traveling internationally. In addition to numerous awards, he received the *CRNI Courage in Editorial Cartooning Award* in 2005, the *Turkish Journalists' Association Press Freedom Award* in 2006 and the *Kofi Annan Courage in Cartooning Award* in 2018. He lives in Istanbul and continues to work on animated cartoons. www.instagram.com/musakart1

Petra Kaster, Deutschland/Germany

Geb.1952 im Ruhrgebiet. Freie Trickfilmautorin, Cartoonistin und Illustratorin. Ihre mehrfach preisgekrönten Cartoons erscheinen in diversen Zeitschriften, Zeitungen (u.a. *Nebelspalter* und *Eulenspiegel*) und Büchern.

Born in 1952 in the Ruhr area. Freelance animator, cartoonist and illustrator. Her award-winning cartoons have appeared in various magazines, newspapers (including *Nebelspalter* and *Eulenspiegel*) and books. www.petrakaster.de

Vladimir Kazanevsky, Ukraine

1950 in der Ukraine geboren. 1973 Abschluss an der Staatlichen Universität Charkow in der Fachrichtung »Kosmische Radiophysik« und 1984 am Institut für Journalismus in Kiew. Seine Zeichnungen wurden in Zeitungen und Magazinen weltweit (u. a. *Nebelspalter, Eulenspiegel*) veröffentlicht. Gewann in 53 Ländern über 500 Preise bei internationalen Zeichenwettbewerben. Aufgrund des Krieges musste Kazanevsky im März 2022 aus seinem Land fliehen. Er erhielt den *Internationalen Preis für Pressekarikaturen* 2022, den *Cartoonists Kofi Annan Courage in Cartooning Award*, verliehen von der Stiftung *Freedom Cartoonist* in Partnerschaft mit *CRNI* und *Cartooning for Peace*.

Born in the Ukraine in 1950. Graduated from Kharkov State University in 1973 with a degree in »Cosmic Radiophysics« and from the Institute of Journalism in Kiev in 1984. His drawings have been published in newspapers and magazines worldwide (e.g. *Nebelspalter, Eulenspiegel*). He won over 500 prizes in international drawing competitions in 53 countries. Due to the war, Kazanevsky had to flee his country in March 2022. He received the *International Prize for Press Cartoons* 2022, the *Cartoonists Kofi Annan Courage in Cartooning Award*, presented by the *Freedom Cartoonist Foundation* in partnership with *CRNI* and *Cartooning for Peace*.

Arkadiusz Krupa, Polen/Poland

Richter seit 2001, derzeit seit 2015 am Unterlandesgericht in Łobez in der Strafabteilung. Seit 2021 Lehrbeauftragter an der Fakultät für Recht und Verwaltung der Universität Szczecin. Aktivist zur Förderung der Kenntnisse zu Recht und Gesetz, besonders bei Kindern, Jugendlichen und Senioren. Außerdem Kolumnist eines Rechtsmagazins und bei Tageszeitungen und Karikaturist auf Facebook, einer Zeitung und in Lehrbüchern.

Judge since 2001; currently at the Lower Regional Court in Łobez in the criminal division since 2015. Since 2021 lecturer at the Faculty of Law and Administration of the University of Szczecin. Activist in promoting knowledge of law and justice, especially among children, young people and seniors. He is also a columnist for a legal magazine and daily newspapers and a cartoonist on Facebook, a newspaper and in textbooks. https://www.facebook.com/SlepymOkiemTemidy

Manjul, Indien/India

MANJUL, geb. 1972, ist ein renommierter indischer Karikaturist, der für seine einfühlsamen und satirischen Arbeiten bekannt ist. Er pendelt zwischen der Mumbai Metropolitan Region (MMR) und der National Capital Region (NCR) in Indien hin und her und trägt als freiberuflicher Künstler zu verschiedenen nationalen und internationalen Publikationen bei.

Born in 1972, MANJUL is a renowned Indian cartoonist known for his insightful and satirical artwork. Commuting between the Mumbai Metropolitan Region (MMR) and the National Capital Region (NCR) in India, he contributes to various national and international publications as a freelance artist. linktr.ee/MANJULtoons

Dorthe Landschulz, Deutschland/Germany

1976 in Hamburg geboren, studierte in Hamburg und Paris Illustration und lebt als freie Cartoonistin in der Bretagne. Ihre preisgekrönten Cartoons (zuletzt 2. Platz beim *Deutschen Cartoonpreis* 2022) erscheinen in Magazinen und Zeitungen wie *taz, Eulenspiegel, SHZ, Le Monde* und seit 2019 wöchentlich im *STERN*. Ihre Cartoons sind auch auf Facebook und Instagram zu finden unter dem Namen *Ein Tag Ein Tier* (Deutsch) und *La Loutre-Rhin* (Französisch).

Born in Hamburg in 1976; studied illustration in Hamburg and Paris and lives as a freelance cartoonist in Brittany. Her award-winning cartoons (e. g. 2nd place at the *German Cartoon Prize* 2022) appear in magazines and newspapers such as *taz, Eulenspiegel, SHZ, Le Monde* and, since 2019, weekly in *STERN*. Her cartoons can also be found on Facebook and Instagram under the names *Ein Tag Ein Tier* (German) and *La Loutre-Rhin* (French). www.facebook.com/EinTageinTier

Mario Lars, Deutschland/Germany

Roland Regge-Schulz, geboren 1964 in Mecklenburg, lebt dort als Grafiker, Journalist, Zeichner und Autor. Veröffentlicht in *Eulenspiegel* und diversen Tageszeitungen.

Roland Regge-Schulz, born in 1964 in Mecklenburg, lives there as a graphic designer, journalist, illustrator and author. Published in *Eulenspiegel* and various daily newspapers. www.schulzenhof.de

Til Mette, Deutschland/Germany

1956 in Bielefeld geboren. Studierte Geschichte und Kunst, Mitbegründer der *taz* in Bremen, lebte über 15 Jahre in den USA, seit 2006 in Hamburg. Seine Cartoons sind vielfach preisgekrönt und erscheinen in Büchern und seit 1995 exklusiv im Magazin *STERN*.

Born in Bielefeld in 1956. Studied history and art; co-founder of *taz* in Bremen, lived in the USA for over 15 years and has lived in Hamburg since 2006. His cartoons have won numerous awards and appeared in books and, since 1995, exclusively in *STERN* magazine. www.tilmette.com

Denis Metz, Deutschland/Germany

1974 geboren, zeichnet schon immer Cartoons. Er lebt auf der Nordseeinsel Baltrum, seine Cartoons sind preisgekrönt und erscheinen u. a. in *Süddeutsche Zeitung, taz* und *Titanic* sowie in Büchern.

Born in 1974, he has always drawn cartoons. He lives on the North Sea island of Baltrum and his cartoons have won awards and appear in *Süddeutsche Zeitung, taz* and *Titanic* as well as books. www.schnabulak.de

MOCK, Deutschland/Germany

MOCK (Volker Kischkel), geb. in Lobberich am Niederrhein. Studium der Freien Kunst an der Hochschule für Bildende Künste in Braunschweig. Veröffentlichungen u.a. in *spiegel-online, STERN, Eulenspiegel, juris-Magazin, patho, Westzeit*. Diverse Preise und Auszeichnungen, u. a. beim *Deutschen Karikaturenpreis, Deutschen Cartoonpreis* und *Deutschen Preis für die politische Karikatur.*

MOCK (Volker Kischkel), born in Lobberich on the Lower Rhine. Studied fine arts at the Hochschule für bildende Künste in Brauchschweig. Publications in *spiegel-online, STERN, Eulenspiegel, juris-Magazin, patho, Westzeit*, and others. Various prizes and awards, including the *German Caricature Prize, German Cartoon Prize* and *German Prize for Political Caricature.*www.mock-cartoons.de

OL, Deutschland/Germany

Olaf Schwarzbach, geb. 1965 in Ost-Berlin, ist Cartoonist und Autor. Er zeichnet u. a. für *Berliner Zeitung, Jungle World, Tip Berlin, N-tv.de* u. a. Zahlreiche Buchveröffentlichungen. 2023 wurde er mit dem ersten Platz des *Deutschen Cartoonpreises* ausgezeichnet.

Olaf Schwarzbach, born 1965 in East Berlin, is a cartoonist and author. He draws for *Berliner Zeitung, Jungle World, Tip Berlin, N-tv.de* and other publications. In 2023, he was awarded first place of *German Cartoon Prize*. www.ol-cartoons.de

Ted Rall, USA

Wurde in den 1990ern bekannt für seine politischen Cartoons im Strip-Format mit mehreren Panels. In der New York Times wurde er zum meistgedruckten Karikaturisten. Ralls Zeichnungen wurden in Hunderten von Publikationen auf der ganzen Welt veröffentlicht, darunter *Rolling Stone, Time, Newsweek, Esquire, The Washington Post, San Francisco Chronicle, Los Angeles Times.* Heute ist er einer der am breitesten gewerkschaftlich organisierten politischen Karikaturisten der USA sowie ein gewerkschaftlich organisierter nationaler Meinungs-Kolumnist.

Became known in the 1990s for his political cartoons in strip format with several panels. He became the most reprinted cartoonist in the New York Times. Rall's drawings have been published in hundreds of publications around the world, including *Rolling Stone, Time, Newsweek, Esquire, The Washington Post, San Francisco Chronicle, Los Angeles Times.* Today, he is one of the most broadly unionized political cartoonists in the U.S., as well as a unionized national opinion columnist. rall.com

Stephan Rürup, Deutschland/Germany

1965 geboren, lebt als freier Cartoonist in Münster. Zeichnet für *Titanic, Welt am Sonntag, Journal Frankfurt, Das Magazin, Pragmaticus, RUMS* und div. Tageszeitungen. 2018 gewann er den *Deutschen Cartoonpreis.*

Born in 1965; lives as a freelance cartoonist in Münster. Draws for *Titanic, Welt am Sonntag, Journal Frankfurt, Das Magazin, Pragmaticus, RUMS* and various daily newspapers. He won the *German Cartoon Prize* in 2018. www.hoeheregewalt.de

Heiko Sakurai, Deutschland/Germany

1971 geboren, studierte Germanistik, Geschichte und Politik in Münster. Lebt und arbeitet in Köln und zeichnet politische Karikaturen für zahlreiche Tageszeitungen.

Born in 1971; studied German language and literature, history and politics in Münster. Lives and works in Cologne and draws political cartoons for numerous daily newspapers. www.Sakuari-cartoons.de

Schwarwel, Deutschland/Germany

Jahrgang 1968, lebt und arbeitet in Leipzig als Illustrator, Trickfilmer, Karikaturist, Comiczeichner, Animator, Storyboarder, Drehbuch-Autor, Regisseur, Produzent, Art Director (*Glücklicher Montag*), Autor und Zeichner.

Born in 1968; lives and works in Leipzig as an illustrator, animator, cartoonist, comic artist, animator, storyboarder, screenwriter, director, producer, art director (*Glücklicher Montag*), author and illustrator. www.gluecklicher-montag.de

Swen, Schweiz/Swizzerland

Silvan Wegmann, geb. 1969, lebt als Karikaturist und Illustrator in Baden, Schweiz. Er veröffentlicht in diversen Schweizer Zeitungen und Magazinen und ist Mitinitiator des Cartoon- und Satirefestivals *bissfest* in Baden.

Silvan Wegmann, born in 1969, is a cartoonist and illustrator living in Baden, Switzerland. He publishes in various Swiss newspapers and magazines and is co-initiator of the cartoon and satire festival *bissfest* in Baden. www.swen.ch

Klaus Stuttmann, Deutschland/Germany

Geb. 1949 in Süddeutschland, seit 1970 lebt er in Berlin. Studierte Kunstgeschichte und Geschichte, seine Cartoons wurden vielfach ausgezeichnet, er veröffentlicht täglich im *Tagesspiegel* und diversen anderen Tageszeitungen.

Born in southern Germany in 1949, he has lived in Berlin since 1970. Studied art history and history; his cartoons have won numerous awards. He publishes daily in the *Tagesspiegel* and various other daily newspapers. www.stuttmann-karikatur.de

Stefano Tartarotti, Italien/Italy

Geboren 1968 in Südtirol, studierte er an der Scuola del Fumetto in Mailand und lebt heute in der Emilia-Romagna. Er ist Comiczeichner, Cartoonist und Illustrator, er hat zahlreiche Bücher und Spiele illustriert, arbeitet außerdem für internationale Werbeagenturen und Zeitungen und Zeitschriften.

Born in South Tyrol in 1968, he studied at the Scuola del Fumetto in Milan and now lives in Emilia-Romagna. He is a comic artist, cartoonist and illustrator and has illustrated numerous books and games. He also works for international advertising agencies, newspapers and magazines. Tartarotti.com

Bas van der Schot, Niederlande/Netherlands

Geb. 1970, ist politischer Karikaturist und Illustrator zwischen Amsterdam und Berlin. Er studierte Politikwissenschaft in Amsterdam, seit 2011 erscheinen seine politischen Karikaturen dreimal wöchentlich in der Tageszeitung *de Volkskrant*, der größten Qualitätszeitung der Niederlande. Seine Arbeiten werden zudem über *Courrier International, Cartoon Movement* und *Cagle* verbreitet.

Born in 1970; he is a political cartoonist and illustrator based in Amsterdam and Berlin. He studied political science in Amsterdam and since 2011 his political cartoons have appeared three times a week in the daily newspaper *de Volkskrant*, the largest quality newspaper in the Netherlands. His work is also distributed by *Courrier International, Cartoon Movement* and *Cagle*. basvanderschot.com

Cathy Wilcox, Australien/Australia

Cathy Wilcox, 1963 in Sydney geboren, preisgekrönte Cartoonistin und Illustratorin. Studierte von 1981 bis 1984 Grafikdesign am Sydney College of the Arts. Von 1985 bis 1987 lebte sie in Paris in Frankreich, wo sie als Illustratorin und Grafikdesignerin für englischsprachige Zeitschriften wie *Paris Passion* und *Speakeasy* arbeitete und Literaturwissenschaft studierte. Seit 1989 Cartoonistin für *Sydney Morning Herald*.

Cathy Wilcox, born in Sydney in 1963, is an award-winning cartoonist and illustrator. She studied graphic design at the Sydney College of the Arts from 1981 to 1984. From 1985 to 1987 she lived in Paris, France, where she studied literature and worked as an illustrator and graphic designer for magazines in English such as *Paris Passion* and *Speakeasy*. She has been a cartoonist for the *Sydney Morning Herald* since 1989. www.cathywilcox.com.au